THE ANDES

The ruins of Machu Picchu on a misty day. To the south are the Salcantay Mountains and to the north the peaks of the Urubamba range.

THE ANDES

by TAKEHIDE KAZAMI

Published by
KODANSHA INTERNATIONAL LTD.
Tokyo, Japan & Palo Alto, Calif., U.S.A.

Distributed in the British Commonwealth (excluding Canada and the Far East) by Ward Lock & Company Ltd., London and Sydney; in Continental Europe by Boxerbooks, Inc., Zurich; and in the Far East by Japan Publications Trading Co., P.O. Box 5030 Tokyo International, Tokyo. Published by Kodansha International Ltd., 2-12-21 Otowa, Bunkyo-ku, Tokyo 112, Japan, and Kodansha International/ U.S.A. Ltd., 599 College Avenue, Palo Alto, California 94306. Copyright © 1972, by Kodansha International Ltd. All rights reserved. Printed in Japan.

LCC   72-183850
ISBN   0-87011-164-7
JBC   0325-783268-2361

First edition, 1972

Contents

Incan Heritage

High up in the Andes Mountains, roads still exist paved by the Incas in the distant past. The Incan emperors must have traveled along these road during their frequent trips of inspection to outlying provinces. These same roads must at times have witnessed the parades of the emperors' victorious armies returning to Cuzco after their battles against rebellious tribes. Perhaps the scene was something like this:

Ahead of the conquering army marches a group of buglars. The sound of their bugles echoes off the high surrounding slopes of the Andes and reverberates back to the milling crowd of men, women, and children who have gathered at the roadside to see the splendid army of the emperor. Following the buglars is a group of soldiers bearing shields and pulling huge catapults. Next comes a band of men armed with axes and stout wooden staffs, followed by men carrying long spears and lances. The main force, however, is composed of the brave array of thousands of soldiers whose breasts are decorated with silver ornaments captured from the enemy. The commanders of the troops can be easily distinguished by their multicolored feather headdresses and epaulets of pure beaten gold.

In stark contrast to this brilliant array of soldiers are the thousands of naked prisoners, their hands tied behind their backs, barely able to walk. In the center of the staggering crowd of prisoners is a large cage containing a naked man—the pitiful figure of the enemy's commander in chief.

There is also a large number of women among the prisoners, and, like the men, they are naked. The jubilant crowd along the road roars its praise of the conquering heroes and exalts in the great power and authority of the emperor. The prisoners are trembling at the thought of the fate that they know will befall them.

The emperor, guarded by hundreds of noblemen, sits high upon a palanquin carried by his men. Around him are piled the gold and silver objects that are the spoils of war. The procession passes slowly through the kneeling crowds of spectators.

No written records have been discovered in any of the regions of the Andes. Therefore, the history of the peoples who lived there can only be pieced together by anthropologists and archaeologists. Even now many fragments of the puzzle are still missing.

At the present time on the highlands of the Andes in Peru, Bolivia, and Chile live a total of six million South American Indians believed to be descended from the Incas. The physical characteristics of these Indians resemble closely those of the Mongoloid races of Asia, leading ethnologists to believe that they came originally from the continent of Asia.

Exactly when the ancestors of the Indians first emigrated to the American continent is not known, but man is thought to have colonized America from Asia perhaps around 25,000 B.C. The route of this migration may have been by a land or ice bridge in the area now covered by the Bering Strait. These people were hunters rather than farmers and probably made the journey in pursuit of game—

for centuries small groups drifted eastward into America, and by 10,000 B.C. many small communities had spread themselves over the habitable regions of the Andes. By about 2500 B.C. the hunters had learned the basic principles of agriculture and had simple tools. It was these early farmers who initiated the habit of terracing the mountainsides, which not only gave them more room, but checked erosion and runoff of the topsoil. By 1200 B.C. the mountain peoples could make their own cooking utensils, mirrors, and beads. They had also learned how to weave—a craft that still flourishes throughout the Andes today.

By the time of the birth of Christ, closely built groups of adobe houses had been established, and an intricate system of irrigation had been established to aid agriculture. Also by this time the strange, and still unexplained, practice of trepanning (drilling holes in the skull to cure illness) had become common. Since the operations were performed with stone scalpels, the survival rate surmised from unearthed skulls is amazingly high.

During the first century A.D. an era of urbanization resulted in large cities planned with a sophistication far in advance of the times. The larger cities were composed of rectangular dwellings with massive walls. Those who worked on the land lived within the cities and went out each day to the farms.

The Incan Empire emerged during the later stages of the long history of the people living in the Andes. They did not call themselves Incas. The name was said to have been given to the tribes who spoke a language called Quechua by the Spanish conquerors, who had heard that they called their leaders "Inca." However, this is only one theory. Another hypothesized that the Incas were a small tribe living near present-day Cuzco who also spoke Quechua. This tribe was thought to have flourished and built a great empire. The people living in this empire then started to call themselves "Incas."

Perhaps the most authoritative theory (propounded by the Incan historian Dr. J. H. Rowe) maintains that the Incas originated in the Lake Titicaca area, since excavated mummies reveal them to have had the short stature and deep chests of a high altitude dwelling people. Dr. Rowe further surmises that the people who invaded Cuzco and established an empire were a backward nation compared to the more civilized coastal population. Nevertheless, on the battlefield they prevailed.

The Incas are famous, among other things, for their lack of a written language. In view of their swift rise to power and numerous technical achievements, this has always surprised scholars. Despite their lack of a written language, however, the Incas did keep complex accounts and records by means of a bundle of elaborately knotted strings called *quipu*. This consisted of a cord to which were tied other lesser cords of diverse colors and in which were tied knots in significant groups and at significant intervals. To these knots might be tied a third class of still smaller cords or threads, which, in their turn, bore knots. The great Inca Pachacuti felt that the *quipu* was such a vital tool that he said, "He who attempts to count the stars, not even knowing how to count the knots and marks of the *quipus*, should be held in derision." The combinations of the *quipu* served as an aid to memory, and were also used in the memorizing of narrative verse, which preserved Incan history and traditions and was passed on to each suceeding generation.

According to available data, the Incan Empire came into being around 1200 A.D. A total of thirteen emperors ruled over the vast empire until the middle of the sixteenth century. Apart from these few facts everything is veiled in mystery—a mystery, of course, that adds fascination to the world of the Incas. So before relating my own adventures in the Andes, let me outline briefly what is known of the Incan myths and legends.

One god stands out above all others in Incan myth. He is Kon-Tiki Viracocha, the creator of the world. He is also the creator of the Incan people and the supreme god who holds sway over the entire universe, according to legend.

Before the Incas appeared in the Andes, a long period of darkness enveloped the earth, and there was no sun. The people prayed to Kon-Tiki Viracocha, the almighty god, to give them back the sun. He heard their prayer, and one day the dazzling sun rose above an island in Lake Titicaca, and light and happiness was restored to the world. This lake, which restored light to the world, is a freshwater lake 12,500 feet up in the Andes. It is the highest lake in the world, 138 miles long, 50 miles wide, and 900 feet deep at its deepest point. It is more like an inland sea than a lake. The eastern shore is Bolivian territory and the western, Peruvian. On its southern shore are located the pre-Incan ruins of Tiahuanaco, built sometime before 1000 A.D.

There are two legends on the subject of who founded the Incan Empire. One of them asserts that Manco Capac and his sister Mama Ocllo were created by the sun god on the Island of the Sun in Lake Titicaca. Obeying the commands of the sun god, Manco Capac, who carried a golden staff, and his sister set out on a journey. They traveled northwards from Titicaca, and after a long and laborious trip finally reached the valley of Cuzco. Manco Capac pushed his golden staff into the ground. It immediately sank into the earth and disappeared. Then they knew they had reached the fertile land promised them by the sun god. Manco Capac taught the existing inhabitants how to farm, while his sister taught the women the art of weaving, and the prosperity of the community increased from that time onwards. Manco Capac also married his sister in the legend, foreshadowing the later Incan custom.

The other legend tells of a small hill called Pacari Tampu about eighteen miles southeast of Cuzco. In the side of the hill were three caves called Tampu Toma, and from the beautiful middle cave emerged Manco Capac, the founder of the Incan Empire. In the Quechuan language Manco Capac means "a most powerful chieftain with absolute authority." Manco Capac is nevertheless only a legendary figure.

The second emperor of the Incas is said to have been called Sinchi Roca Inca. He seems actually to have existed and was a powerful leader and a brave warrior. The third in line was Lloque Yupanqui ("left-handed wise man"), who is said to have had a long life. His son was called Mayta Capac ("strong and powerful chieftain"). He had an aggressive character and was constantly waging war. It is he who is said to have subjugated all the tribes living around Cuzco. He was also the first emperor to initiate the custom of making inspection trips throughout his domain. This custom was followed faithfully by his successors and became one of the most important functions of an emperor. His legendary attributes also include his skill as a stonemason, his construction of numerous grand buildings, and even the engineering of suspension bridges.

The fifth emperor was Capac Yupanqui ("wise chieftain"), about whom little is known. The next and sixth emperor, Inca Roca, was known as "the strong and courageous Inca." He also made many military conquests. His successor, Yahuar Huakak ("the man who shed tears of blood"), was supposedly a cowardly emperor.

The eighth in the dynasty was Viracocha Inca ("white-colored and noble Inca"). He is said to have been one of the most outstanding emperors in Incan history. It was he who devised a plan to subjugate all the lands and tribes surrounding the Incan Empire. Under his leadership the Incas made conquest after conquest. Also during the reign of Viracocha the Incan religion of worshiping the sun began to spread far and wide.

To the west of Cuzco was the country of the Incas called Quecha, and further west was another region named Chanca. These two countries were destined to war against each other. The Chancas were a people who formerly dwelt in jungles—a rapacious but brave race. A great battle was fought in Cuzco, the Incan capital, between the Chancas and the Incas, resulting in the latter's victory. The Chancas fought the Incas several more times after this but were always defeated. In time the Chancas were absorbed into the Incan Empire. The location of the capital of this once powerful Chanca state is still not known.

The ninth emperor of the Incas was Pachacuti Inca Yupanqui ("a wise Inca who carries out great reforms like an earthquake"). He was the most famous of the Incan emperors, reigned from 1438–71, and possessed all the qualities of a great ruler. It was he who reconstructed Cuzco after the ravages of the wars against the Chancas. He built temples to the sun god and established a centralized system of government as well as various social reforms, greatly expanding the power and influence of the Incan Empire. In addition to the temples dedicated to the sun god, he also constructed a temple for virgins. Worship of the sun god became an absolute creed, and the emperor also came to be worshiped as the incarnation of the sun god.

THE ANDES

The wife of the Inca was called *qoya* ("star"), and was usually his full sister. She often played an important, though unofficial, role in the state, and was beloved by the people. Beneath the Inca and his *qoya* in the social hierachy came the *allyu*. These were a type of clan, each descended from illegitimate children of the Inca, and the members held important posts in the government of the empire. The *allyus* in turn grouped themselves into provinces. Although the *allyus* held land in the empire, it was as a courtesy from the state. Private ownership of land was unknown in the Incan Empire. The land was divided into three parts: one part supported the people of the *allyu*; one part benefited the state; and yet another division was set aside for the church.

Pachacuti, after putting his own kingdom in order, waged war on numerous other tribes, from the Vilcabama on the lower reaches of the Urubamba River to the north, to the Vilcas and Soras to the west, and the Aimaya to the south. He even sent expeditions to the Cajamarca district far to the north. Pachacuti also developed agriculture and initiated public engineering projects. It was during his reign that the art of Incan stonemasonry reached its zenith, and numerous colossal fortresses were built.

There was no system of currency in the Incan Empire, and all taxes were collected in labor. This made possible many of the gigantic building projects. The head of each household was called a *puric*, and he had to cultivate his own land and do his share of cultivating the state's land and the church's land. Members of the ruling class of the Incas were exempt from this collective labor, but worked for the state in administrative capacities instead, as a kind of elite civil service.

As the territories of the Incan Empire expanded, a great network of roads was constructed. From Cuzco, the capital, roads radiated in all directions as the result of Pachacuti's vision and effort. Stations were established at strategic points in the empire, and messengers transmitted the orders of the emperor to distant provinces through these stations, which were the only effective means of communication within the Incan Empire at that time. The messengers also gathered important information from all provinces for the emperor. To maintain his power, it has been surmised that Pachacuti had a standing army of more than seventy thousand men.

His son, Topa Inca, helped his father rule the empire. At times, Topa Inca led great expeditions to places as far away as Quito in Ecuador. He also conquered the great Chimu Empire on the northern coast of Peru, which was very powerful at that time. After a long reign Pachacuti relinquished his throne to his son Topa Inca in the year 1471 A.D. During the thirty-three-year reign of Pachacuti, the Incan Empire had expanded fourteenfold.

Topa Inca, the tenth sovereign, led his army through the tropical swamps in the east and conquered the tribes living there. He advanced to the Titicaca district and destroyed two states on the highland of Aimaya. He pushed forward from Bolivia into Chile as far as the Maule River and made it the southernmost boundary of his empire.

The fortress of Sacsahuaman in Cuzco was also completed by Topa Inca, whose reign was long (1471–93) and contributed substantially to the advancement of culture and politics and the reinforcement of the empire's armed forces. Topa, the first Inca to establish the custom of marrying his sister, had eighty sons and thirty daughters by his numerous concubines. Of his two sons who were legitimate, he designated Kushwarpa to succeed him as the eleventh emperor of the Incas. As soon as Kushwarpa was enthroned, he changed his name to Huayna Capac ("young and virtuous chieftain"). It was during his reign that the territory of the Incan Empire expanded to its maximum. The northern border of the empire was the Ankusmajo River in Columbia. The southernmost border was the Maule River in central Chile. The Incan Empire then covered a total area of three hundred eighty thousand square miles and the breadth of the empire from north to south was an incredible two thousand five hundred miles.

Just before he died, Huaya Capac heard the news that whiteskinned strangers had appeared at the border between Bolivia and the Incan Empire. The year was 1523, and this was the first time the Incans had come into contact with Europeans. The news of the white men's arrival plunged Capac into deep apprehension. According to Incan legend, Kon-Tiki Viracocha, the god of creation, was fair skinned, and when the country was in grave danger, legend said he would reveal himself and save the nation in its crisis.

Francisco Pizarro, the Spanish conqueror, is often described as the first white man to discover the Incan Empire. In fact, there was another European who had previously glimpsed the Incan Empire from Bolivia. He was Alejo Garcia, a Portuguese, and he did see the Incan civilization before Pizarro.

Five years after the death of Huayna Capac in 1525, the Incan Empire was divided by internal conflict. Capac had two sons, one of whom was the son of Capac and his empress, the other the child of his concubine. The former was named Huascar and the latter Atahualpa. These two sons of Capac fought each other in competition for the throne and vast territories of the Incan Empire.

Huayna Capac died suddenly in Quito in an epidemic of plague, and he had no time to make the usual formal announcement of his successor, although he had intended his son Huascar to be his heir. Huascar was consequently crowned at Cuzco by the high priest as the twelfth Incan emperor. Atahualpa, who was in Quito, assumed the governorship of Quito and the northern provinces and also the command of the army that had been accompanying Huayna Capac when he died in 1525.

The two sons of Huayna Capac fought with each other incessantly, but in a great battle at the town of Cajamarca in the north central highlands, Atahualpa's army won a final and complete victory over Huascar. Atahualpa was then crowned the thirteenth emperor of the Incas. It was around this time that men with pale faces and long beards—the so-called Viracochas—made their appearance once again. It was the year 1532, and the Viracochas were in fact a squad of Spanish soldiers led by Francisco Pizarro. Pizarro sent his half-brother Hernando together with a young captain named Hernando de Soto to invite Atahualpa to visit the Viracochas' headquarters. Atahualpa, accompanied by several thousand soldiers, paid Pizzaro a visit on 16 November 1532, but Pizarro met the Incan emperor with an ambush, blew the emperor's soldiers to pieces with cannon, rode down the remnants with cavalry, and took Atahualpa prisoner.

Atahualpa was confined in a small dark stone room in Cajamarca and was ordered to pay a ransom for his freedom. He agreed to fill his cell with gold and two other rooms with silver as his ransom. Messengers were dispatched throughout the Incan Empire to gather the treasures of the land. It is said that the ransom collected and distributed to Pizarro and his men was worth more than twenty million dollars.

THE ANDES 🐗

On 29 August 1533, Atahualpa was converted to Christianity and baptized Juan. Then he was summarily executed in the public square by strangulation the very same day. With Atahualpa's death, the great Incan Empire ceased to exist.

On 12 November 1533, the victorious Pizarro entered Cuzco, the capital of the Incas. He was accompanied by a total of only four hundred officers and men. Cuzco was a treasure-house of gold, silver, and precious stones. Even after the great ransom for Atahualpa had been collected and brought to Pizarro in Cajamarca, a large number of bars, figurines, and jars of pure gold were still left in the colossal stone palace of the emperor in Cuzco. These treasures were looted by the Spaniards, melted down, and distributed among the enraptured troops.

Francisco Pizarro, who had been appointed governor-general of Peru by the Spanish monarchy, built a new capital in Lima on the Pacific coast and transferred his headquarters there.

Five years after the conquest of the Incas, Pizarro and his longtime friend and comrade-in-arms, Diego del Almagro, quarreled. In April 1538, Almagro gathered five hundred men around him and challenged the authority of Pizarro. In an internecine battle, Pizarro's troops were victorious and Almagro was captured and put to death by the coldblooded Pizarro, despite his former friend's impassioned plea for his life. But Pizarro himself was destined for a similar fate. On 26 June 1541, he was assassinated in his house in Lima by raiders led by Diego, Almagro's son. Pizarro is thought to have been sixty-five when he was killed.

Francisco Pizarro, the conqueror of the Incas, was a colorful figure. He was born in the village of Trujillo in southern Spain, probably around the year 1471. Numerous legends exist about this

Spanish overlord of Peru. One maintains that Pizarro was born into a poor family and spent his youth as a swineherd. More concrete is the fact that in 1515 he joined Vasco de Balboa's expedition, which discovered the Pacific Ocean. Perhaps inspired by this venture, when tales of the splendor of the Incan Empire reached his ears, Pizarro decided to stake his fortune and his life on conquering the Incas.

In November 1524, Pizarro sailed for the fabled land of the Incas. He was plagued by heavy storms and eventually ran short of food. He arrived finally at the island of Gallo (Hunger Island) and there he made his now famous speech to his men. Drawing his sword, Pizarro drew a line in the earth and exclaimed:

"My friends and fellow comrades-in-arms! South of this line lie untold hardships and starvation, treacherous reefs and storms, bitter wars and even death; but there also the golden land of the Incas awaits us. North of this line lies peace—but the peace of poverty. Fellow comrades, which side of the line do you choose? I myself will take the south."

So saying Pizarro crossed over the line to the southern side. However, only thirteen men followed his example. After facing great peril, Pizarro and these thirteen men reached Tumbes on the Peruvian coast between February and March of 1527.

Meanwhile, Atahualpa in Quito learned that Pizarro, who had been appointed governor-general of Peru by the Spanish, had gathered his men and left his base on the Peruvian coast on 24 September 1532. On 15 November that same year, Pizarro entered the town of Cajamarca where the fortress palace of Atahualpa was located. Pizarro's forces consisted of 110 infantry, 76 cavalry, 13 guns, and 20 bows. The next day the ambush already described took place in the town. The capture and subsequent public strangling of the Emperor Atahaulpa sounded the death knell of the glorious Incan Empire.

After the death of Pizarro at the hands of assassins led by Almagro's son Diego, in 1541, the succeeding governors-general of Peru appointed by the Spanish monarchy did not hesitate to destroy the great culture in the highlands of the Andes. The colonial policy of Spain was little but plunder and destruction.

During the eighteenth century a series of rebellions arose among the oppressed Indians of the Andes. From the middle of the same century independence movements elsewhere in South America gained increasing momentum. The first country to proclaim its independence from Spain was Bolivia in 1809, followed by Argentina and Colombia. Argentina's brilliant rebel leader General Jose de San Martin came to lead Peru in her struggle for freedom and together with Simón Bolivar of Venezuela achieved independence for Peru in 1824.

That, briefly, is an outline of the history of the Incan Empire to its thirteenth and last emperor, Atahualpa, the destruction of the empire by the Spanish led by Francisco Pizarro, to Peru's eventual independence. Now let us embark on a contemporary journey to the Peruvian Andes, and try to unravel the threads of the ancient and the modern.

Mountain Cities of Today and Yesterday

It was summer in the Peruvian capital when I flew into Lima one day in early December 1969. I found it essentially a Spanish city. Three centuries of Spanish rule have overlaid any vestiges of Incan culture. The name of the city is derived from the River Rimac, which bisects the city. Rimac means "the river that speaks," which is an appropriate name for a tumultuous, tumbling torrent that descends 12,000 feet in eighty miles. The general atmosphere in Lima is as casual and leisured as any Mediterranean town—156 days in the year (including Sundays) are holidays. Much of this leisure the populace devotes to the traditional sport of bullfighting. Lima boasts the oldest bullring in South America, the fourth oldest in the world, where the first fight was held on 22 February 1566. In addition to bullfighting, cockfighting also flourishes.

The title "City of Kings" is supposed to have been a legacy from Pizarro, who first established the capital there. The square in the center of the city is named after General San Martin, who led the independence struggles, and the city radiates out from this square. Another square called the Plaza de Armas, laid out in 1535 by Pizarro himself, still retains the atmosphere of Spanish colonial days and today is shown to tourists as typifying Spanish influence. The most ancient building in this square is the Great Cathedral, built in the middle of the seventeenth century. In a small chapel within the cathedral is a glass coffin containing the supposed remains of Francisco Pizarro, the conqueror of the Incas, with the skull delicately attached to the skeleton with silver wire. Next door is the town hall, where the first charter of the city of Lima can be seen. It is signed by Pizarro with his mark, since he could not write his name.

It almost never rains in Lima, and there is no need for umbrellas. One strange sight resulting from this, which I saw from the top of a tall building, was a great number of roofless houses, whose inhabitants could see the blue sky and the blazing sun above their heads. The white walls of the houses and their beautiful Spanish-style bay windows ornamented with wooden carving are at their best when viewed in the sparkling sunlight.

As I walked through the streets of Lima, I came across numerous churches and religious buildings, which were the products of the early stages of the Spanish colonial period. The elaborate monastery of La Merced with its five cloisters is thought to have been built in 1535. The monasteries and nunneries were a flourishing part of the Lima community under Spanish rule. Most of the education and health care emanated from the religious foundations.

Despite this heritage of beauty, the city has not escaped the troubles of the twentieth century. I was disappointed by the terrible exhaust fumes and raucous engine noises emitted by the secondhand American buses as they rattled their way through the streets. Another unnerving sight was the large number of dilapidated taxis called "collectives," overflowing with passengers but looking as though they belonged on a scrap heap.

A friend of mine told me of a common saying about Peru: "The biggest evil in the country is the thieves and after them the police," and I did notice while in Lima a large number of policemen idling around in the streets. Four or five of them would stand at a street corner passing their time gossiping. They did not appear to be making any effort to direct the traffic. I saw a policeman in the Plaza de Armas sitting in a telephone booth leisurely reading a book.

As a result of the discomfort of high altitudes, the slum district in Lima, like La Paz in Bolivia, is located on the hills surrounding the city. The worst slums, called the Barrieras, are rows of gray adobe hovels without any kind of drainage, which house three hundred thousand people. Open tanks at intervals provide the only source of water. The problem is of mammoth proportions, and as yet Peru is without the resources to house the slum dwellers elsewhere.

Lima is justly famous for its museums and archaeological collections. The Art and Archaeology Museum has a large collection of Incan and pre-Incan artifacts. I also visited the Rafael Larco Herrera Museum renowned for its collection of ceramics, especially of the Mochican period. These pieces of unglazed pottery date from around 600 A.D. and are among the most interesting of the sixty-thousand-piece collection.

In the Cathedral of San Francisco, thousands of urns containing human bones, mostly of Indians, are kept in the cathedral crypt, and the very walls are hung with human bones, giving the place an eerie atmosphere.

After staying several days in Lima, I took a jet to Cuzco, accomplishing the journey in only fifty-five minutes. I was sorry that clouds obscured the snow-covered peaks of the Andes, but as we ap-

THE ANDES

proached Cuzco, visibility improved somewhat and I could see the white peak of Salcantay with its glacier to my left—a beautiful mountain rising 20,551 feet above sea level. The green valley at the foot of the mountains was dotted with red-roofed houses, seen as the plane circled the mountains to land in Cuzco, a city located 11,000 feet up in the Andes.

What are they like, the Andes Mountains, in which the Incan civilization blossomed and grew? The name is thought by some to be derived from the Incan word *anderes* meaning the terraces that the Incas built on the sides of the mountains; others maintain that the Quechuan word *anti*, meaning east, is the origin of the name Andes.

The Andes is a four thousand-mile-long mountain range that runs parallel with the Pacific coast of South America from the Isthmus of Panama in the north to Cape Horn near the Antarctic. It is one of the greatest mountain ranges in the world, with numerous peaks of more than 18,000 feet in height. The highest peak, Aconcagua, rises 22,835 above sea level and is also the highest mountain in the southern hemisphere. It is sometimes called the Guardian of the Andes. On the Pacific side of the mountains is desert terrain, but the further east one climbs, the more rain falls. A great plateau unfolds at an altitude of 12,000 feet, which is known as *puna*. Peaks towering more than 18,000 feet with numerous glaciers have created many lakes on this *puna*. On the eastern side of the range is a deep valley filled with equatorial jungle in which is the source of the Amazon River. The district of the central Andes, which was the cradle of Andean civilization and the Incan Empire, has a fairly clement climate and is peopled by a variety of different tribes.

The mountains are rich in mineral resources. Gold and quartz are found in Colombia; Peru and Chile have silver-bearing copper deposits; and Bolivia is rich in tungsten and tin. Mining these mountain riches is fraught with difficulty, and the railroads of the central Andes climb higher than any others in the world. The highest human habitations in the world are also found here, where some shepherds live in huts built at 17,000 feet.

Having passed over some of these awe-inspiring mountains, I reached Cuzco, said to be the most ancient city in South America. During the thirteenth to sixteenth centuries when the Incan Empire flourished, Cuzco was the sacred city of the Incas and the center of the Incan Empire. Here was the imperial palace, home of the Inca. Today it is a busy city, 11,480 feet up in the mountains with a population of eighty thousand.

The word *cuzco* means "center" or "navel," so the name of the city aptly described its role in the empire. But when Pizarro conquered Cuzco in 1534, the town was transformed under Spanish colonial rule. A total of twenty-three Catholic churches were built by the Spanish conquerors. The stone-paved streets of Cuzco, however, are still reminiscent of the heyday of Incan power and evoke nostalgia for the glory of the bygone empire.

The narrow, stepped streets are more suitable for animals than automobiles, and llamas are often seen hard at work. The llama, the alpaca, the guanaco, and the vicuna are all native to Peru. The llama and the alpaca have been domesticated for several hundred years, and a few vicunas and guanacos roam wild in the Andes today. These animals can live at an altitude of more than 9,000 feet and are invaluable to the Indians. The llama in particular is of great value because of its flesh, its fur, and its adaptibility as a beast of burden. No uncommon sight is a caravan of more than fifty llamas transporting goods and produce to marketplaces several hundred miles away. The alpaca is a smaller animal, but its fur is of finer quality than that of the llama. But the vicuna has the most valuable fur and because of this has been reduced almost to extinction—it is now protected against hunters.

At the center of Cuzco is the Plaza de Armas, surrounded by the Great Cathedral, the Church of Compania, and stone houses with Spanish-style balconies. Part of the stone foundation in the Church of Compania is said to have been the site of the palace of the eleventh Incan emperor, Huayna Capac, although the facades of both churches were reconstructed after the disastrous earthquake of 1650.

On the opposite side of this imperial palace was the temple of the sun with its attendant virgin priestesses. On 15 November 1533, Pizarro and four hundred of his men entered the capital of Cuzco, and are reputed to have brutally raped these Incan virgins. Built on the foundations of this sun temple is the Church of Santo Domingo, said to be the oldest monastery in Peru.

The Spanish conquerors frequently made use of the stone foundations of Incan buildings when they built their own cathedrals and churches. Ironically during the great earthquake of 1650, practically all the Spanish-built churches were destroyed, but the Incan foundations survived intact, demonstrating once again the high level of Incan skill in stonemasonry.

Although the Incan temples have been converted into Catholic churches, the atmosphere of the Incan Empire can still be seen in other ways in Cuzco. The brilliant costumes of the Indians have changed little over the centuries. The skirts of the women are especially beautiful. They wear a large number of skirts on top of each other, and the larger the number of skirts, the higher their social status. The numerous folds of the skirts also play an important role in keeping the wearer warm—the hips of a woman wearing six or seven skirts take on gigantic proportions.

I was particularly interested in the various types of hats worn by the women: white silk hats, black derby hats, colored hats, etc. Married women wear hats with black ribbons hanging from them, while unmarried girls in Cuzco wear hats of brilliant colors. In some other provinces, unmarried women wear hats decorated with flowers. Practically all the clothes worn by the women they make themselves. The men's costumes are as colorful as the women's. Clothes differ according to provinces in the color and pattern of the ponchos, the kind of hat, and the length of the trousers.

The Indians living around Cuzco, like those in the central and northern Andes, speak a language called Quechua. Most of the five million inhabitants of Peru can probably speak this extremely complex language.

The central market of Cuzco in front of the station is open every day. On the stone-paved road a variety of goods and products are displayed: vegetables, fruit, grain, meat, other foodstuffs, and clothes. The marketplace is full of people, but the atmosphere is strangely subdued. The vendors and customers do not raise their voices when haggling over the price of the goods. It is also noticeable that the vendors, squatting down on the pavement waiting for prospective customers, are all women.

Before the Spaniards introduced coins, goods were exchanged by a barter system. This system is still operative in provincial marketplaces even today. The goods have dual prices. For example, five onions could either be bought for one sol (about three cents) or exchanged for five handfuls of barley. The marketplaces in the provinces are also social meeting spots. Farmers congregate there to rest their tired bodies after a week's work and to swap gossip with their friends.

The marketplaces, as always, furnished me with numerous interesting subjects for my camera, as did the colorful costumes of the Indians. One day while driving along in a jeep, I photographed a woman we passed. She immediately thrust out her hand and stridently demanded money. My driver shouted at her, "What do you mean 'money'? You have only yourself to blame for sitting down in such a public place!" This was not an isolated incident. I was frequently asked for money when I tried to take pictures.

I saw two old women and their children in the slum district of Cuzco spinning yarn from llama wool and weaving Incan-style ponchos. The spindles and looms they were using were hand operated, like those I had seen in remote villages in the Himalayas. I asked them if I could take their picture, but the reply was negative. Persuasion was of no avail: the women were most obstinate. I took out my purse, but discovered to my annoyance that I had no small change. I then told the women that I would bring them the money the next day, but they still refused. After much haggling, however, I managed to get my pictures and then handed one of the women a bill. In a businesslike manner she went into her house and returned with the change.

While visiting Cuzco, I was often told that the Spanish did not leave any treasures in Peru. They drained the country and exploited the people. They also undermined the social and legal structure of Incan society, leaving the Indians with few loyalties and little sense of identity.

Near Cuzco are the ruins of the great Incan fortress of Sacsahuaman, which was built over a period of eighty years by some thirty thousand laborers. The work was begun in 1140 in the reign of the ninth emperor, Pachacuti Inca Yupanqui, who initiated many such building projects. J. Alden Mason, an expert on Andean archaeology, said of the ruins, "Certainly no other archaeological structure in the two Americas gives the visitor the awesome impression of stupendousness that Sacsahuaman does," and as I surveyed the vast structure I felt he was probably right. The upper part of the fortress no longer stands because the Spanish invaders used its stone to build Catholic churches. Only the lower portion of the fortress remains today. The layers of stone are an unbelievable nine hundred feet thick, and the biggest single stone is twenty-seven feet high, fourteen feet wide, and twelve feet thick. The stones are fitted together with such a degree of accuracy that not even a razor blade can be inserted between them. The Incas did not have pulleys, but they did understand the principle of the lever and the fulcrum. The also used a kind of crane to raise the huge masses of stone. To quarry the stone they used hard stone tools as well as bronze implements. The purpose of the gigantic fortress is not clear, since it is not strategically placed for defence. It may have been a refuge for the people if attacked by neighboring tribes, since it is honeycombed with underground passages and chambers where women and animals may have been hidden for safety.

The stone was transported to the site from a quarry some twenty miles away. How this was done is still a mystery, and many questions about the huge fortress remain unanswered. Near the square where the ruins are located, I saw a herd of llamas peacefully munching grass. An Indian boy who happened to be passing posed for me shyly, bringing the past and the present into photographic juxtaposition.

THE ANDES

From Cuzco I traveled to Pisac, an ancient fortress city about twenty miles east of Cuzco. The market, which takes place every Sunday, is famous. Sold here are colorful Indian clothes, ponchos, and hats as well as a variety of foodstuffs brought in by Indians from outlying districts. The market is usually thronged with tourists, and the brilliantly colored clothes are, in fact, from the shops in Cuzco. I found the secondhand furniture and implements on sale more interesting. My attention was soon caught by an old painted wooden cup. After bargaining with the vendor for several minutes, I suceeded in purchasing it for less than half the asking price.

On the mountain above the marketplace are the ruins of an Incan town. I climbed up to them and came to a stone terrace, which was used as a military lookout in Incan times. Nearby were the ruins of an observatory.

We then drove along the side of the Urubamba River down the Pisac Valley and came to yet another set of Incan ruins. Ollantay-tambo is a half-completed Incan fortress built on the side of a mountain. Six enormous slabs of red porphyry, twelve feet long and five feet wide, lay on the ground. It is thought that they were once part of a temple. Higher up were five buildings, one above the other, with steep roofs, once grass-thatched, where the virgins of the sun are supposed to have had their dwellings and school.

After completing our tour of these ancient ruins, we drove along the mountain road. I noticed a group of women drinking something out of large cups beside the road and I asked the driver what they were drinking. He told me it was *chicha*, an alcoholic drink produced from corn, which has been made in the area for the last two thousand years. The drink is produced by steaming corn, chewing it, mixing it with saliva, and then fermenting it. When I approached the group with camera in hand, I found them in a convivial and cooperative mood, perhaps from the effects of the drink.

Machu Pichu, the greatest mystery of the Incan Empire, is located in a deep valley of the Urubamba River. The ruins were discovered on 24 July 1911 by a young American archaeologist called Hiram Bingham, who followed up rumors told him by his Indian guide of a city hidden in the mountains. His discovery was the most dramatic archaeological find in the history of the Andean civilizations.

An express train runs daily from Cuzco to Machu Picchu. It is a fast diesel train carrying only tourists. The distance between Cuzco and Machu Picchu is seventy miles, which the train covers in three hours. This train leaves Cuzco every morning at 7:10 A.M. Another, slower train for ordinary citizens leaves Cuzco at 7:30 A.M. I requested the surprised stationmaster in Cuzco to let me ride, at least one way, on the ordinary train, which carries Indian passengers and stops at every station between Cuzco and Machu Picchu. Each time we stopped at a station, villagers brought basketfuls of farm produce and other goods to sell to the passengers on the train. The Indian passengers were themselves burdened with heavy loads of assorted goods, since they had gone to Cuzco from the villages along the railway to exchange their produce for city wares.

Black smoke poured from the train as it made its way from the Cuzco Valley up into the mountains. The conductor came to check our tickets, but nevertheless numerous Indians managed to get a free ride. These stowaways did not seem the least bit put out by the arrival of the conductor, and invented ingenious stories to explain their ticketless condition. Some of them told the conductor that they were friends of employees working at Cuzco station. This reminder of the extreme poverty of the majority of South American Indians was reinforced by the ragged clothing of the mother and child sitting opposite me.

There are no platforms at the intervening stations. Villagers rushed up to the train as it pulled into the station and tried to sell us vegetables, fruit, and fried pork. They even boarded the train to sell their goods. They did not seem perturbed when the train left the station, but merely rode along to the next station and got off there.

The lower reaches of the Urubamba River turn into a red, swiftly flowing current near the station of Machu Picchu, which lies in the bottom of a deep valley. We left the train and a small bus took us up the valley. When it had crossed a bridge, the road suddenly began to twist and turn, and a new driver replaced the first one. This new driver seemed to be a newcomer to his occupation, and we were nervous about this amateur driver for there were a total of thirteen hairpin bends in which the road mounted 1,500 feet. As the bus climbed the road, the engine responded with what I can only feel were sounds of loud protest.

When we arrived at the hotel, the substitute driver turned into a clerk at the font desk and began accommodating the guests. The ruins of Machu Picchu, which we had all come to see, remained undisturbed for nearly four hundred years, from the time the last of the Incan emperors, Atahualpa, was strangled by the Spanish conquerors. Who constructed this fortress city of Machu Picchu? When was it built? The answers to these questions are shrouded in mystery, and even the original name of the city is still not known.

Outside the fifteen-foot-high wall surrounding the ruins was a cluster of houses, which I was told had been farmers' dwellings. The nobles had lived within the walls. The slopes of the mountains were covered with hundreds of *anderes* (terraced fields) with irrigation ditches running through them, demonstrating how the Incas had managed to feed themselves in such infertile mountainous country.

There seem to have been four sacred temples in Machu Picchu. The most important was the temple of the sun, which is half destroyed, with its three remaining walls facing the main square. Another sun-related temple houses the sundial known as Inti-huatana. *Inti* means "the sun" and *huatana* means "to tie." The sundial itself is composed of square stone pillars set up on an altar. The temple of the half-moon is so called because of is shape. Built on a large rock with a cave in its interior, the half-moon-shaped temple is also called "a tower to thwart the enemy," and has walls of great beauty. Finally on the opposite side of the square is a temple that has three windows. Accoding to Hiram Bingham, the three windows symbolized the three caves called Tampu Toma, although other experts disagree.

In 1912, a total of 143 mummified bodies were discovered in the caves at Machu Picchu, of which 102 were those of young women, 7 were girls, 5 were infants, and 17 were those of adult men. (The remaining 7 were unidentified.) Why were there so many young women among the dead? Were these mummified bodies of virgins of the sun, priestesses of the Incan religion? A prosaic explanation is that the men were killed elsewhere in battle, leaving a mainly female population. But a more fanciful legend says that when the emperor and his soldiers abandoned the city to go forth to battle, the virgins were executed in order to preserve the secret of the city for eternity. And even today the ancient city of Machu Picchu (which means simply "old peak") does not easily yield up the secrets of its history.

THE ANDES

I stayed at Machu Picchu for four days and was profoundly impressed by the magnificence and scale of the ruins. I strolled through the ancient city in both morning and afternoon, and when the mists lifted caught glimpses of the Urubamba Range, as well as the snowcapped mountains of the Salcantay range.

On returning to Cuzco, I wandered about the historic ruins near the city and took many photographs. It was the time of the Inti-Raymi Festival. Formerly this was a festival for the sun god and was one of the most important rituals performed by the Incan emperors. Every year on 24 June, this ritual was held to give thanks for the harvest and to pray for a good harvest the following year. The sun god was all-powerful in the Incan Empire, but today the religious connotation of Inti-Raymi has disappeared.

During the festival the square in Cuzco is filled with dancers, bands, and brilliantly costumed men and women from the villages near the city participating in parades. In the afternoon, more than fifty thousand people gather at the Sacsahuaman Square to witness a reenactment of the ancient ceremonial. Drinking a great deal of home-brewed *chicha*, the Indians spend the whole day in a relaxed and holiday mood.

Lake Titicaca and La Paz

There are only two trains a week from Cuzco to the town of Puno on the shores of Lake Titicaca. The journey takes a whole day, but I did not take the train. Instead I hired a taxi, because I wanted to take photographs of the landscape during the journey. There is a taxi company in Cuzco that provides a car and driver if paid the fares of five passengers. We had requested the driver of our car to come to our hotel at six in the morning, but to our surprise, he was there at five. He was a happy-go-lucky young man with little sense of time, as we discovered later.

We left Cuzco in a cold morning mist. Our driver drove at great speed, leaving clouds of dust in the car's wake. According to the map, the distance between Cuzco and Puno is 233 miles. The young driver evidently wanted to reach Puno as quickly as possible and have time for a long rest there. We passed trucks loaded with goods and a great many Indians sitting on the freight, their faces covered with dust. The trucks seemed to do double duty as unofficial buses.

The lovely Cuzco Valley was green and fertile. It was here, according to Incan legend, that Manco Capac's golden rod sank into the ground, telling him that he had reached the land promised to him by the sun god. As we were driving through the valley, a huge black cow lumbered across the road so suddenly that we bumped into it. The cow was knocked unconscious, and the little girl looking after it began to wail. Without hesitation our driver drove on, and continued for quite a way before stopping to inspect the damage to his car. Having done so, he drove on again quite nonchalantly. I was nonplussed by his casual attitude, but I later learned that if he had stopped at the site of the accident, he would have had a hard time placating the hostile villagers who would have quickly gathered around. The headlights and the door of the car were somewhat damaged, but the car still managed to keep moving. When we reached the next town, the car was put into a repair shop, and we waited there for about two hours.

We then continued on along the Urubamba River, which narrowed suddenly as it neared its source. Then we came to an extensive high plateau and above its desolate expanse we could see the snow-capped peaks of the Andes. We saw herds of llamas pastured here as well as a llama caravan transporting goods to some distant marketplace. The road reaches its highest altitude of 13,000 feet at Vilcanota Pass. The surrounding mountains are all more than 15,000 feet high.

Beyond this pass we came out onto another vast highland plateau. There is no such thing as smog up in this dry and rarified atmosphere; the air is clean and fresh, giving crystal clear visibility into the distance. We stopped for a rest in the town of Juliaca, not far from Puno, and ate our lunch. A market was under way in the town, and the marketplace was full of Indians wearing colorful ponchos and hats. Our driver told us that he would come back in an hour and disappeared into the town with a friend. After lunch we went to the marketplace, took a number of pictures, and made some purchases to wile away the time.

However, our driver failed to return after the hour had elapsed, and I thought of my luggage still in the trunk of the car. Two hours later he made his appearance, not in the least perturbed. He calmly told us that he had gone to the house of his girl friend, had eaten lunch there, taken a bath, and had an afternoon nap. The audacity of his excuse made it difficult to stay annoyed, and we were soon once more on our way.

From Juliaca to Puno stretched a splendidly paved road. On our left side lay the fabled Lake Titicaca. Puno, the administrative center of the province, is a town full of steep hills located on the western shore of the lake, 12,650 feet above sea level, with a population of approximately twenty thousand. The other shore of the lake is Bolivian territory. The distance between the Bolivian port of Guaqui and the Peruvian port of Puno is sixty-five miles. Ships of three thousand tons ply between the two ports. Puno is also the intersection of the railway lines from Cuzco and Arequipa.

Over the millennia, the Indians have adapted physically to enable them to live and work at these extremely high altitudes, at which most people become breathless and inactive. Their lungs are larger than normal, and each oxygen-absorbing sac is fully dilated. They have two quarts more blood than lowlanders, and their hearts are twenty percent larger, with a slower pulse rate. I, of course, had no such physical aids for the high altitudes, and when I strolled through Puno that evening, I found the air so rarified at 12,650 feet that I had difficulty in breathing.

The marketplace was bustling, and for the first time I had the rare opportunity of seeing the tall hats worn by the Maymara tribesmen and women. The people living in the districts surrounding this lake speak three languages, I discovered: Quechua, Aimaya,

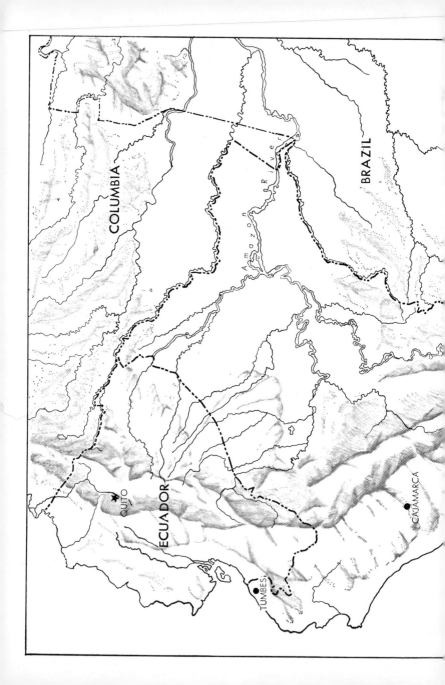

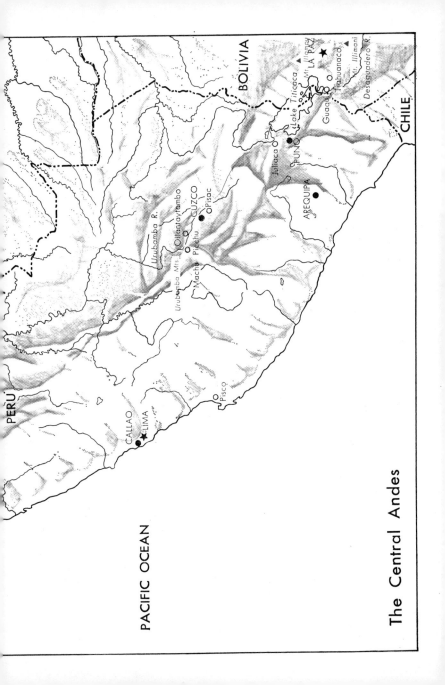

The Central Andes

and Spanish—the latter is spoken only by an upper-class minority.

Titicaca is the highest freshwater lake in the world—some 12,500 feet above sea level. In 1961 the waters of the lake began to recede, and the level is said to have dropped by some eleven feet. The local residents explain that this phenomenon has been caused by cracks in the bottom of the lake created by numerous earthquakes.

On the Peruvian side of the lake, trout have been released into the waters to improve the quality of the fish population. To protect the newly released fish, fishing was prohibited when we visited the lake. However, on the other side of the lake, the Bolivian fishermen were catching these same trout. Their excuse was that they could not help catching the fish if they would swim over to their side.

Lake Titicaca is the home of many Incan myths and legends, including that of the birth of the founder of the empire. Almost legendary themselves are the people of the Uros tribe, a branch of the Maymara tribe, which now has seriously dwindled in number. They build floating islands with a reed called *totora*, and transport earth to these islands so that they can raise vegetables. *Uros* means "lice," and the tribesmen consider themselves to be animals rather than human beings. With these same *totora* reeds they build boats called balsas.

It takes from five to six months to prepare one balsa. After the long curing and drying period, a bundle of dried *totora* reeds are placed on the ground and then tightly woven into three spool-shaped strips. The two thickest ones are used for the sides of the boat, and the remaining thinner one forms the bottom. The life of these painstakingly constructed craft is short—a mere six months.

We saw few trees growing in the vicinity of the lake, only reeds, perhaps due to the high altitude. The people who live on the shores of the lake would be in an unfortunate predicament without the multipurpose *totora* reed.

One morning I hired a boat and visited a floating island of the Uros people. As we crossed the lake we saw a number of balsas, but when I turned my camera on them, the boatmen paddled hurriedly away. Then we landed on one of the floating islands, but when I tried to take pictures of the residents, I was rudely asked for money. I did not mind paying to take their photographs, but the people seemed unnecessarily hostile, which saddened me. I have since heard that the Indians are renowned for never laughing out loud. The Uros tribesmen not only did not laugh, but hardly spoke to us.

The *totora* sails of the balsas turned gold in the rays of the setting sun and were indeed a beautiful sight, but, despite the beauty of their surroundings, the people of this fast-vanishing tribe live an austere life of hardship in their reed-built world.

The following day, we drove to Lake Sillustani, about six miles west of Lake Titicaca. According to legend, the area around Titicaca is thought to have been the burial ground of the leaders of pre-Incan civilizations. The hills around Lake Sillustani were also burial grounds on which still stand stone grave towers called *chullpa*, the resting places of unknown emperors. We drove to the foot of one of these hills and climbed up on foot. From the summit we could see the blue waters of the lake beneath us, dotted with balsas. On the distant hills were more *chullpas*, perhaps as many as a hundred. The height of the *chullpa* towers apparently reflects the status of those buried beneath them. The interiors of the towers are filled with rubble, and bones are strewn around the graves. No grave offerings have been found, presumably due to the intervention of grave robbers.

THE ANDES 🐗

Again the questions went through my mind. How many emperors are buried beneath these hills? When did they reign supreme over the tribes of ancient Peru? All that remains of their glory are these stark stone towers, standing deserted in the thin air. As the evening deepened, I suddenly felt the eerie atmosphere of the place and wanted to flee from these ghosts of the past.

I stayed in Puno for several days and then decided to go on to La Paz, the capital of Bolivia. So I requested the bellboy at the hotel to hire a taxi for me. I was scheduled to depart at six in the morning, and when I reached the car, to my surprise I found the same boy sitting beside the driver. "What are you up to?" I asked the boy. "Please let me ride as far as La Paz," he pleaded. He already seemed to have made an arrangement with the driver, so I acquiesced.

The rain had stopped, and the sky was a deep blue. Lake Titicaca seemed like a great sea. Indians in colorful costumes were herding flocks of llamas. It was a primitive but wonderful sight, and despite the weight of my camera, I hurried off to take more photographs. The air was so thin that the burden of my camera equipment made breathing difficult. The altitude must have been more than 14,500 feet.

We soon reached the Desaquadero River, which marks the border between Peru and Bolivia. The officials checking our passports on the Peruvian side operated out of a bar. When a number of passports had been collected, they disappeared into another room behind the bar, but soon came back saying that everything had been completed.

In front of the bridge leading into Bolivian territory was a border barrier, which blocked our view of Bolivia. I was told that since it was Christmas Day, everyone was on holiday. This made me rather anxious, but my driver went into the office building and soon returned saying, "It's all OK." Evidently he had given some kind of tip to the men in the office. I noticed that the boy from the hotel was not in his seat. Of course he had no passport, so had taken a more devious route and was already inside Bolivia.

The barrier was lifted and we drove into Bolivian territory. In a small office were two soldiers. They looked at our passports, but I had no idea what action they might take. My driver had a brief talk with them, and one of the soldiers jotted something down in a large notebook. It was a description of my occupation and read "schoolboy." I had returned to schoolboy status at more than fifty years of age. It seemed so hilarious that I wanted to say something, but the driver winked at me, so I remained silent. After completing these rather strange entry formalities, we drove on and soon saw the hotel boy, who had bypassed officialdom, waiting for us by the roadside.

We drove east for about twelve miles from the southern shore of Titicaca and reached the ruins of Tihuanaco, where once a pre-Incan civilization flourished. It is a bleak spot lashed by rain and snow on a highland some 13,000 feet above sea level. I found it difficult to imagine that a great civilization had existed here in the ancient past.

Tihuanaco is said to be the capital of a lost kingdom some ten to twelve centuries old. The ruins are 3,000 feet long and 150 feet wide. The so-called Gate of the Sun is the most famous monument of the ruins. It is ten feet high and is carved from a single block of stone weighing ten tons. This stone is thirteen feet long and ten feet wide. I was told that this huge stone had split into two in 1908. The figure of a god is sculpted in the center of the stone. The god's outstretched hands are in the act of destroying two grotesque serpents. Birds are flying to the right and left of the central figure. The carving is beautiful and remains another Andean archaeological mystery.

Many statues of human figures have been excavated from Tihuanaco. The largest of them is now located in a square in La Paz. It stands twenty feet high, and was excavated by an archaeologist named Bennett in 1932. Children everywhere around the ruins of Tihuanaco begged me to buy small stone pumas and bronze decorations with beautiful carvings. They make a living selling these "genuine" artworks to the tourists.

Along the Bolivian shores of Lake Titicaca lives a tribe called the Aimaya who, in a pre-Incan era, ruled a powerful kingdom called the Aimaya Empire. A great capital city took the temple at Tihuanaco as its center. This empire too was eventually subdued by the Incas in the reign of the fifth emperor, Capac Yupanqui.

As we approached La Paz, on our left we saw the mountains of the Cordillerra Apolobamba capped with snow, contrasting sharply with the red earth of the desolate Altiplano plateau. The airport at La Paz is located on a highland 13,358 feet above sea level with runways almost four miles long, since the planes take longer to land in the thin air. Below it the city nestles in the valley. La Paz, population 470,000, is a city built in a bowl high up in the Andes Mountains. Apart from being the capital of Bolivia, it has claim to fame as the highest city in the world. The Altiplano plateau is located at the widest point of the Andes range, and is thirty miles wide at an altitude of between 9,000 and 12,000 feet. It is the very roof of South America, and despite the height and the dryness of the air, two-thirds of Bolivia's population live there. The people are poor, and the conditions of life are hard. The per capita income in Bolivia averages around one hundred dollars a year, which is among the lowest in the world. Bad conditions and high altitudes take a severe toll of health, and the Indians have a life expectancy of only thirty-two years. Economically the country is heavily dependent on tin, which constitutes eight percent of the nation's budget, two-thirds of its export earnings, amounting to twenty-five percent of the whole world's supply of tin.

Bolivia is named after its hero, General Simón Bolivar, who came from Venezuela to defeat the Spanish at Tumusula and gain independence for Bolivia in 1825. La Paz, of course, means "peace," but ever since the first revolution occurred in Latin America, far from being at peace, Bolivia has witnessed a total of 179 revolutions and changes in government in the course of 126 years. As a result of this political turmoil, Bolivia is often called "a beggar sitting on a chair of gold," for the country is rich in mineral resources, yet some two-thirds of the population are still indigenous Indians leading poverty-stricken lives.

The city of La Paz is surrounded by great Andean peaks including Illampu (21,276 feet), Huayna-Potosi (19,988 feet), and Illimani (22,579 feet), the second highest peak in Bolivia. At this great height the air of the city is deficient in oxygen, and fires are so rare that there is not even a fire station in the whole city. The quality of the air is also the reason that the rich live principally in the lower districts of the city where the air is denser, and the poor congregate in the hilly sections. The air, too, prevents the police from running in pursuit of thieves or criminals—the paucity of oxygen forces them to take their time. In a city so full of lung-stretching hills even the dogs stroll along in a leisurely manner.

About twenty miles from La Paz is the world's highest cosmic ray observatory. It is on Mount Chacartaya at an altitude of 15,760 feet. Above the observatory are skiing grounds with a ski lodge and lift. Again this is the world's highest skiing area, with the beautiful Mount Huayna-Potosi soaring up beside it. Far to the west, Lake Titicaca shines like a blue mirror in the middle of the desolate Altiplano.

The visit to La Paz brought to an end my Andean journey. While there I took numerous mountain photographs, because mountains have always had a deep emotional appeal to me. Not only the mountains have this appeal, but also the primitive people living among them, leading practically the same lives as their ancestors for generations past and still fighting for their meager livelihood despite the encroachment of modern civilization

When I look over the pictures I took of the central Andes and the people there, I recall them with nostalgia, and my thoughts return to those now distant mountains with their compelling mystique and colorful inhabitants.

1. *The Plaza de Armas* in Lima, capital of Peru. In one corner stands the statue of Francisco Pizzaro, who subdued the Incan Empire in a decisive battle on 16 January 1532.

2-3. *Soldiers on guard* in colorful uniforms in front of the official residence of the president in the Plaza de Armes. The changing of the guard takes place with punctilious ceremony at nine o'clock each morning.

5. *Spanish-style bay windows* are frequently to be seen in Lima. Pictured here is part of the Great Cathedral with the black, wooden window in striking contrast to the cream-colored stone building.

4. *Spanish colonial influence* is clearly revealed in the Plaza de Armas with the Great Cathedral at its center. The mummified body of Pizzaro reposes in a glass coffin within the cathedral.

6. *In the courtyard* of a Spanish-style house, the ornamented wood and white walls blend harmoniously. This old house is squeezed between new, modern buildings, a not unusual sight in many-faceted Lima

7. *Religious art* is a prominent feature ▶ of Lima. Beautifully decorated old churches and chapels appear at every turn.

◀8. *Lima Museum*, where archaeological finds, art objects, and textiles of the pre-Incan and Incan periods are displayed.

9. *Carrying images of Christ*, devout Catholics walk through the streets of Lima under the blazing midday sun.

10. *Lima*, known as the "town of kings," was originally built by Pizzaro. Since July 1821, when Peru became independent of Spain, the city has grown and expanded. It now bears few traces of the former ancient city.

11. *Sandy beaches* near Lima are crowded with sunbathers and strollers, but rarely with swimmers. The Humboldt Current flowing from Antarctica makes the water too cold for comfort.

12. *The ruined city of Pachacamac* in the sub-
urbs of Lima was occupied by the Incas.
Before their conquest it was a temple city

dedicated to the god of creation, Pachacamac—*pacha* means "heaven," and *camac*
"creator."

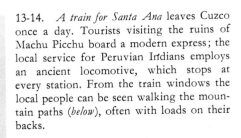

13-14. *A train for Santa Ana* leaves Cuzco once a day. Tourists visiting the ruins of Machu Picchu board a modern express; the local service for Peruvian Indians employs an ancient locomotive, which stops at every station. From the train windows the local people can be seen walking the mountain paths (*below*), often with loads on their backs.

15-17. *The local train* from Cuzco to Santa Ana was loaded with unofficial passengers without tickets. The intermediate stations had no platforms, and when the train stopped it was immediately surrounded by droves of villagers selling every kind of food.

18-19. *Cuzco* is a city of steep hills. The stepped streets date from the time of the Incas, who did not use the wheel. The Peruvian Indians journey to Cuzco with their produce packed on the backs of llamas.

20. *A pedestrian* takes a brief rest on the curb in a street that has changed little since the days of the Incas.

21. *This young couple*, selling their wares in the fascinating back streets of Cuzco, willingly posed for the camera.

22-23. *It is mostly the Indian women* everywhere who are hard at work selling fruit and vegetables. Whenever I photographed them, they would immediately ask for money.

◄24. *Schoolgirls* returning home pass in front of the Great Cathedral in the Plaza de Armas.

25-27. *The cemetery in Cuzco* is set on a hill from where there is a good view of the houses of the town. The graves of the ordinary citizens are marked by simple white crosses, but those of the rich (*opposite*) are like miniature apartment buildings with glass doors, and are sometimes elaborately decorated.

71

28. *Cuzco*, the sacred city of the Incas, is the oldest town in South America. Situated at an altitude of ten thousand three hundred feet, it has a population of about one hundred thousand.

29. *A beautiful landscape* on the outskirts of Cuzco.

30. *A wide plateau* in the Urubamba Valley. The snowcapped Andes still glisten in the late afternoon sun, while Indian children herd their sheep past the facade of an old, stone church.

31. *Women weaving ponchos* on looms similar to those used by the Incas. The woman standing is spinning the yarn—it takes about three months to complete a poncho.

32. *A Peruvian Indian woman* in a tall hat comes down the village street with her child on her back. The women usually put anything they want to carry on their backs, leaving their hands free.

33. *The ruins of Ollantaytambo*, in the Urubamba Valley about forty-two miles north of Cuzco, are the remains of a half-completed fortress of the Incan Empire.

34. *A herd of llamas* tended by a mother and her daughter graze on the hillside above the fortress of Sacsahuaman. The altitude here is about twelve thousand feet.

35. *Sacsahuaman* is the largest of the ▶ numerous Incan fortresses. Thirty thousand laborers are said to have toiled for eighty years to build this fort at the command of the tenth Incan emperor, Topac Yupanqui.

36. *Wide highlands* north of Cuzco are excellently irrigated and the scene of flourishing agriculture. The chief product is potatoes.

37. *The hardworking women* of the ▶ South American Indians are on the whole taciturn, but at the same time seem quite gay.

38. *Women at the roadside* drinking ▶ what my driver told me was "a home brew" seemed in high fettle.

40. *The village master* (*left*) carries a ▶ silver-embossed staff to denote his position of authority. The boy blows on the conch-shell horn to announce the arrival of the village master.

39. *In Pisac*, a small town nineteen miles north of Cuzco, this father and his children had walked four or five hours to attend the morning market. The bundle on the right is a bashful girl who dived under her poncho when she saw the camera.

41. *The women's hats* indicate what ▶ province they come from. Unmarried girls wear colorful dresses, while married women wear black ribbons.

42-45. *The market at Pisac* is held every Sunday and attracts crowds from miles around. Goods are bought or bartered—five onions may cost either one sol or five handfuls of barley. Indian clothing made in Cuzco is on sale, but the prices seemed to be beyond the reach of all but the tourists.

46. *Machu Picchu* in the Quechuan language means "an old mountain." This lost city, flanked by two mountains, lay undiscovered until the American archaeologist Hiram Bingham visited the place in 1911.

47. *A vendor* selling fruit juice to tourists takes a rest in front of the rock walls of the Machu Picchu ruins.

48. *Interior of the main temple* within the fortress at Machu Picchu. The amazing stonework done by the Incas can be seen here—a razor blade cannot be inserted between the stones.

49-53. *The Andes moutain range* runs along the west coast of South American for fifty-six hundred miles. Many South American Indians live in the highlands, supporting themselves by agriculture and raising llamas and alpacas.

55. *Children* are the first to gather ▶ around curiously in any part of the world.

54. *Llamas* are the only animals that can graze in this Andean wasteland at an altitude of twelve thousand feet. They were domesticated several hundren years ago and both supply flesh and hair and act as pack animals. Llamas are a member of the camel family.

56. *The stone-paved streets* of this ▶ village are deserted in the heat of the midday sun.

57-58. *Puno* is a town on the Peruvian side of Lake Titicaca and is located at an altitude of around twelve thousand five hundred feet. Men and women from the Aimaya tribe come in their tall hats to the morning bazaar.

60-63. *Lake Titicaca*, the largest freshwater lake in South America, borders both Peru and Bolivia. The Uros tribesmen (*uros* means "lice") build floating islands on the lake with *totora* reeds. They then cover these islands with dirt and grow vegetables on them. Boats called balsa are also made from these reeds. The Uros say that the lake was created from the tears of their women. Titicaca is 112 miles long, 50 miles wide, and 900 feet deep.

64-66. *Lake Sillustani*, shown below, is situated about six miles from Lake Titicaca. The hills around the two lakes are reputed to be the burial ground of leaders of a pre-Inca culture. Giant stone monuments mark the graves (*opposite*).

67-68. *The ruins of Tiahuanaco* on the Bolivian side of Lake Titicaca mark all that remains of the capital of a kingdom that flourished here two thousand years ago. Its history is still shrouded in mystery. Opposite is the Gate of the Sun on which are sculpted the figures of gods.

69. *La Paz*, the highest city in the▶ world, lies eleven thousand feet above sea level. Because of the lack of oxygen in the air, the rich live in the lower parts of the city and the poor higher up the mountains.

70-71. *Flowers* bloom around small lakes in the La Paz district (*previous page*), despite the severity of the environment. The formations towering above the lakes (below) have been eroded into cathedrallike spires and buttresses.